NORMAN ROCKWELL

Paintings

WINGS BOOKS

New York • Avenel, New Jersey

Copyright © 1994 by Random House Value Publishing, Inc.

Grateful acknowledgment is made to the Norman Rockwell Family Trust for permission to reproduce all of the images in this book.

All images are copyrighted by the Norman Rockwell Family Trust.

All images in this book, as well as the front and back cover, were supplied by the Norman Rockwell Museum at Stockbridge, Massachusetts. Grateful acknowledgment is made to the museum for permission to use their transparencies of the artwork.

This 1994 edition is published by Wings Books,
distributed by Random House Value Publishing, Inc.,
40 Engelhard Avenue, Avenel, New Jersey 07001.

Random House
New York • Toronto • London • Sydney • Auckland

Printed and bound in Malaysia

Library of Congress Cataloging-in-Publication Data

Rockwell, Norman, 1894–1978.
    Norman Rockwell : paintings.
       p.   cm.
    Includes bibliographical references.
    ISBN 0-517-11921-8
    1. Rockwell, Norman, 1894–1978. I. Title.
  ND237.R68A4   1994
  759.13—dc20   94-20390
                           CIP

8 7 6 5 4 3 2

"Some people have been kind enough to call me a fine artist. I've always called myself an illustrator. I'm not sure what the difference is. All I know is that whatever type of work I do, I try to give it my very best. Art has been my life." [1]

—NORMAN ROCKWELL

1. *No Swimming*
   1921

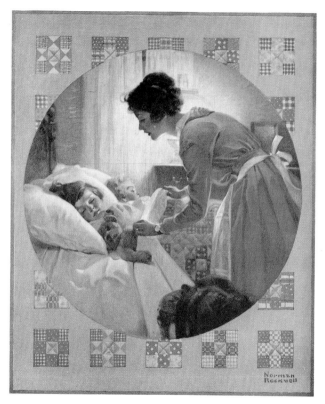

2. *Mother Tucking Children into Bed*
   1921

3. *Doctor and Doll*
   1929

4. *The Law Student*
   1927

5. *Marriage License*
   1955

6. *Saying Grace*
   1951

7. *Breaking Home Ties*
   1954

8. *Checkers*
   1929

9. *Boy in a Dining Car*
   1946

10. *Rural Vacation*
    1938

11. *Norman Rockwell Visits a Family Doctor*
    1947

12. *Girl with Black Eye (Shiner)*
    1953

12. *Girl with Black Eye (Shiner)*
    1953

11. *Norman Rockwell Visits a Family Doctor*
    1947

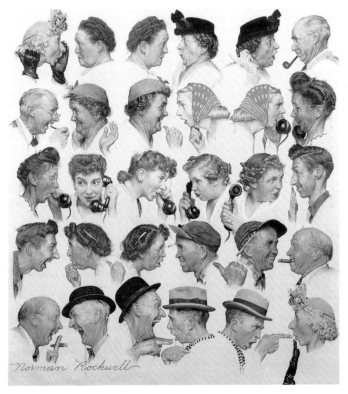

13. *The Gossips*
    1948

14. *Welcome to Elmville*
1929

15. *Rosie the Riveter*
    1943

16. *The Deadline*
    1938

17. *Going and Coming*
    1947

18. *Main Street Stockbridge at Christmas*
1967

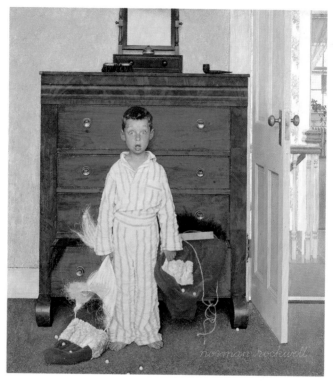

19. *The Discovery*
     1956

20. *Christmas Homecoming*
    1948

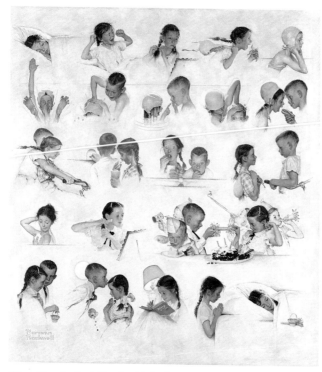

21. *Day in the Life of a Little Girl*
    1952

22. *Girl at Mirror*
    1954

23. *Freedom of Speech*
    1943

24. *Freedom of Worship*
    1943

25. *Freedom from Want*
1943

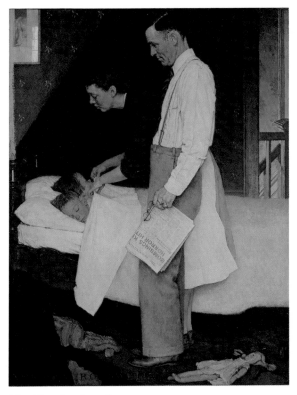

26. *Freedom from Fear*
    1943

27. *The Day I Painted Ike*
     1952

28. *Portrait of JFK*
    1960

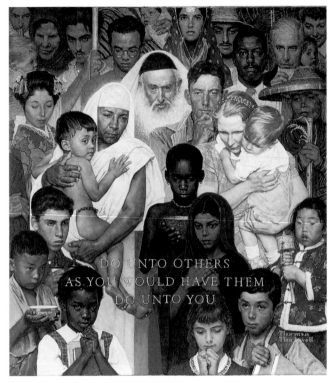

29.   *The Golden Rule*
      1961

31. *Triple Self-Portrait*
    1960

30. *The Problem We All Live With*
    1964

Afterword

For over sixty years, through two world wars, hard times and boom years, the cold war and the civil rights movement, the turbulent sixties and the sobering seventies, Norman Rockwell created a panoramic record of much that is fundamentally unique to America. No other artist can claim a body of work that so brilliantly captures on canvas—with humor and pathos, affection and grit—the character of a people.

Norman Percevel Rockwell, the younger of two brothers, was born February 3, 1894 on New York's upper West Side. His maternal grandfather, Howard Hill, was a moderately successful painter of detailed nature studies. His father, Jarvis Waring Rockwell, was an excellent amateur artist, who enjoyed copying illustrations from books and magazines. Father and son shared this pastime and the young Rockwell began to develop his considerable drawing skills at a very young age. He and his father also enjoyed reading aloud from the classics. As early as age nine, Rockwell began using his imagination to visualize and then illustrate scenes from his favorite books—one of the first pictures he drew was of Mr. Micawber from *David Copperfield*.

In 1903 the family moved to Mamaroneck, New York and Rockwell began a lifelong love affair with the country—particularly summers in the country, a theme that would dominate many of his adult paintings. The idealization of boyhood was an ironic choice for Rockwell who, as a child, often found himself the odd man out with his peers. He was underdeveloped, unathletic, pigeon-toed, and wore corrective shoes and eyeglasses. Never good at sports, he entertained his friends by sketching chalk drawings on the streets.

Rockwell knew he wanted to draw for a living by age 12. In 1909, at the age of 14, he began attending art classes part-time at the Chase School. He dropped out of high school in his sophomore year to study art full-time at the National Academy, but soon enrolled in the more liberal Art Students League.

Rockwell was only 17 when he illustrated his first book, the *Tell Me Why Stories*. He left art school a year later to become a full-time professional, painting the illustrations for at least four novels. When he was 19, Rockwell was offered the position of Art Director for *Boys' Life*, the official magazine of the Boy Scouts, and in the following two years, he produced over 150 illustrations for the magazine, the *Boy Scout Hike Book*, and the *Boy Scout Camp Book*. This was the start of a lifelong association between Rockwell and the Boy Scouts, one that lasted over six decades.

The year 1916 marked several turning points for Rockwell. He married his first wife, Irene O'Connor, and settled into the urbane, suburban lifestyle of New Rochelle, where he would live and work for the next twenty years. As he began doing more work for adult magazines and illustrations for advertisements, he also started to develop a very specific painting style and technique.

On May 20, 1916, at age 22, Rockwell's first *Saturday Evening Post* cover appeared. "Boy with Baby Carriage" shows a young boy dressed in his Sunday best, begrudgingly wheeling a younger sibling's baby carriage past two jeering friends on their way to play softball. The cover was an instant success. It embodies themes that would dominate Rockwell's paintings and illustrations for the next fifty years, specifically youth and adherence to family values; humor and life's embarrassing moments.

The triumphs and travails of growing up are depicted in *No Swimming* (plate 1), *Breaking Home Ties* (plate 7), *The Discovery* (plate 19), and a series of paintings featuring one of Rockwell's favorite young models, Mary Whalen—*Girl With Black Eye* (plate 12), *Day in the Life of a Little Girl* (plate 21), and the touchingly poignant *Girl at the Mirror* (plate 22). Youthful love is celebrated in all its innocence in *After the Prom* (front cover).

Humorous renderings of everyday life and its embarrassing or uncomfortable moments may be seen in *Welcome to Elmville* (plate 14)—a very early take on the small-town "speed trap," and in *The Gossips* (plate 13), where Rockwell and his wife are included among the array of neighborhood busybodies.

Old-fashioned patriotism and traditional values are extolled in *Rosie the Riveter* (plate 15) and the Four Freedoms' series (plates 23-26), while history-in-the-making is recorded in *The Day I Painted Ike* (plate 27) and *Portrait of JFK* (plate 28).

Rockwell was also fascinated with the "dimension of time," with painting what has *just* happened or *will* happen. This theme is marvelously realized in his two-part *Post* cover, *Going and Coming* (plate 17). There are obvious and subtle changes in these scenes of a family going on vacation, then returning home. Only Grandma—who has seen and done it all—remains stubbornly stoic throughout both trips.

The juxtaposition of old age and youth was one of Rockwell's favorite devices. This theme runs like a delicate thread through some of his finest works, from early illustrations like *Doctor and Doll* (plate

3) and *Rural Vacation* (plate 10), to the masterfully rendered *Marriage License* (plate 5) and his most popular "generational" painting, *Saying Grace* (plate 6).

With these works, Rockwell became the *Saturday Evening Post*'s top cover artist. His illustrations appeared in the weekly magazine until 1963, and from 1919 until 1943 he produced many of the Christmas covers.

Each Rockwell painting was created with rigorous attention to detail, from the first tiny "idea sketches," to a series of more fully rendered charcoal drawings and color studies. Much time and energy went into finding the most appropriate models, props, and costumes. The final oil paintings show a strong sense of contour—Rockwell emphasized the outer edge of each part of a painting so that objects are never lost in shadow. His subjects are placed head-on or in profile, so that they appear to be "up close" to the viewer. He also used, with great effect, the technique of "foreground invitation," a device to bring the viewer "into the picture."[2] A dramatic example of the use of foreground invitation can be seen in *Freedom from Want* (plate 25), where the open end of the table in the foreground "invites" people to the meal.

The decades of the 1930s, '40s, and '50s brought major changes to Rockwell's personal life and public work. He and Irene Rockwell were divorced in 1929. The following year, Rockwell met and married Mary Barstow. They were together for 29 years and had three sons, Jarvis, Thomas, and Peter. The Rockwells made a series of moves—from New Rochelle to Vermont in 1939, and then to Stockbridge, Massachusetts in 1953.

Rockwell turned a creative corner in 1935 and began producing some of his best and most personally satisfying works: the critically-acclaimed illustrations for Heritage Press's special editions of *Tom Sawyer* and *Huckleberry Finn*; a brilliant series of magazine illustrations, including those for the life of Louisa May Alcott in *Woman's Home Companion*, and, between 1936 and 1939, some of his most famous *Post* covers.

During World War II, Rockwell painted numerous illustrations in support of the war effort, but none compared to his interpretation of the Four Freedoms, which President Franklin Delano Roosevelt presented in a speech in 1941. The War Department initially turned down Rockwell's idea of illustrating the Four Freedoms in everyday scenes with which people could easily identify; he even offered to do the paintings for free. The *Saturday Evening Post*, however, was thrilled with his concept and featured the paintings as full-page illustrations inside the magazine, together with essays by important Americans discussing each of the Freedoms. By his own account, this was the most difficult job Rockwell had ever undertaken. *Freedom of Speech* (plate 23) and *Freedom of Worship* (plate 24) were particularly challenging and he redid each of them at least four times.[3] They became his favorites. All four paintings use a commonplace setting to frame a single idea: the varied and respectful attitudes of listening in *Freedom of Speech*; the reverential study of praying hands in *Freedom of Worship*; the open-ended invitation to share a meal in *Freedom from Want*; and the stark contrast between peacefully sleeping children and a violent newspaper headline in *Freedom from Fear* (plate 26).

Over 20,000 fans wrote to Rockwell after the publication of the Four Freedoms. The War Department then toured the four original paintings around the country, where they were viewed by almost a million and a half people and helped raised over $130 million dollars in war bonds.[4]

The last twenty years of Rockwell's life were marked by major changes. Mary Rockwell died suddenly in 1959. Two years later, Rockwell married Molly Punderson, with whom he would spend the remainder of his life. In the same year, he painted the beautiful and stirring *Golden Rule* (plate 29), for which he used his neighbors and local students to depict the diverse nationalities. In 1969, he painted one of his few still lifes, *Spring Flowers* (back cover), an ode to Molly, who was a passionate gardener.

Rockwell left the *Post* in 1963 after a 47-year partnership. He immediately went to work for the more contemporary *Look* magazine and many of his illustrations for them are starkly realistic in subject matter.

It is often said about Rockwell that he always avoided the "sordid and unpleasant" but this appears to be a broad overstatement. Perhaps it would be more correct to say that he imbued his later, more serious paintings with the same detail, dignity, and deceptive simplicity that marked his early works, and that "his portrait of the nation remained, as always, more benevolent than deserved."[5] Even the latter may be too broad a statement. Rockwell's first illustration for *Look* detailed the explosive issue of school desegregation. *The Problem We All Live With* (plate 30), painted in typical Rockwell style, shows a small African-American child, flanked by four large and faceless federal marshals, walking past a wall smeared with tomatoes, a racial epithet, and the carved initials of the Klu Klux Klan. There is nothing "benevolent" about this illustration. It is a powerful indictment of racial intolerance.

Critics have begun to reexamine Rockwell's art, assessing his qualities as a gifted painter, rather than cataloging his output as a prolific illustrator. It seems not enough, then, to label Rockwell only as an optimistic celebrant of what life could or should be. A great number of Rockwell's paintings certainly celebrate the quixotic American character—equal parts innocence and devilry, wit and pathos, bravado and humility. Yet many of his personal artistic heroes painted a darker side of life. In *Triple Self-Portrait* (title page), Rockwell surrounds himself with the works of those painters from whom he drew lifelong inspiration. Among them are Picasso and Van Gogh, equally revered for their stylistic innovations and their social commentary—qualities that apparently meant much to Rockwell the painter.

Norman Rockwell died in 1978, at age 84. Shortly before his death, at a celebration in his honor, he had remarked, "Maybe the secret to so many artists living so long is that every painting is a new adventure. So you see, they're always *looking ahead* to something new and exciting. The secret is not to look back."[6] Viewing his work in its totality, perhaps no truer description of it can be given—it always moves forward. A fitting epitaph for America's most famous and enduring painter.

NOTES

1. Donald Walton, *A Rockwell Portrait: An Intimate Biography* (Kansas: Sheed Andrews and McMeel, Inc., 1978), 7
2. Thomas S. Buechner, *The Norman Rockwell Treasury* (New York: Galahad Books, 1992), 18
3. Walton, 161
4. Ibid, 162
5. Buechner, 104
6. Walton, 283-284

List of Plates

All of the photographs in this book were supplied by the Norman Rockwell Museum at Stockbridge, Massachusetts:

The Norman Rockwell Museum at Stockbridge

The Norman Rockwell Museum at Stockbridge, founded with the help of Norman and Molly Rockwell in 1969, is dedicated to the extraordinary career and enduring art of Norman Rockwell. Located in the small Massachusetts town he called home for the last twenty-five years of his life, the museum is home to Rockwell's own collection of his work, left in trust to the museum in 1973, along with the artist's studio and archives, and has the largest collection of Rockwell art in the world. Using the Rockwell collection as a framework, the museum's exhibitions and programs explore Rockwell's work within the larger cultural, social, and political context of his lifetime while also examining the power and impact of the art of illustration. Highlights of the collection include Rockwell's *Triple Self-Portrait, Stockbridge Main Street at Christmas,* and the *Four Freedoms,* Rockwell's contribution to the war effort based on the themes expressed by Franklin D. Roosevelt during World War II.

P.O. Box 308
Route 183
Stockbridge, Massachusetts 01262
(413) 298-4100